STEP INTO READING®

2

STEP

READING WITH HELP

A SCIENCE READER

Have No Fear!
Halloween Is Here!

by Tish Rabe

based on a television script by Patrick Granleese

illustrated by Tom Brannon

Random House 🏠 New York

"Nick," Sally said,
"I love Halloween!
And that's the *best* spider
I have ever seen!"

"Sally," said Nick,
"what we need to do now
is go find some costumes,
but I don't know how."

"I do!" said the Cat.

"I know where to find

costumes for us

that are one of a kind.

We need to go now,
and we need to be quick."
"Yes—we need to be home
before dark," added Nick.

"Have no fear!" said the Cat.

"Come along. Follow me!

I know how to get there.

Come now, you will see."

Suddenly they heard
a chattering sound.
Everyone stopped.
They looked all around.

"That sound," Nick said,
"it came from in there.
Is it a monster?
A tiger? A bear?"

Then something flew out.
They all jumped a mile!
"Say, I *know* that bat,"
the Cat said with a smile.

"Sally and Nick,
meet my friend Batty Bat."
Batty flew down,
and he said, "Hello, Cat!"

"Batty," the Cat said,
"and other bats I have known
often chatter at dusk
before they leave home.

Bats are mammals that fly.

They like insects to eat.

Bats sleep during the day—

they hang by their feet!"

"We are here," Sally said,
"to find costumes today."
"Follow me!" Batty said.
"Flying is the best way."

So they started to fly,
but they saw a bright flash.
"Cat!" Sally said.
"Are we going to crash?"

"We are not," said the Cat.
"There is nothing to fear.
That is only some lightning.
It is far, far from here.

In fact, we have made it!
Look there, up ahead.
We are going to that
spooky house," the Cat said.

They flew to the house,
and each one got to pick
their favorite costume.
"We did it!" said Nick.

"These are the best costumes
we have ever seen!
Now we are ready. . . .

"Happy Halloween!"

Have you read these Step into Reading books?

STEP **2** READING WITH HELP

Put a check next to each one you've read!

Are you ready for the next Step?

STEP **3** READING ON YOUR OWN

For activities, information about Common Core, and more books to read, visit
StepIntoReading.com

STEP INTO READING®

Halloween is the time for spooky fun! The Cat in the Hat will show you how it's done!

Learning to Read, Step by Step!

1 Ready to Read Preschool–Kindergarten

2 Reading with Help Preschool–Grade 1
Does your child recognize familiar words on sight and sound out new words with help? Step 2 is just right.
Basic Vocabulary • Short Sentences • Simple Stories

3 Reading on Your Own Grades 1–3

4 Reading Paragraphs Grades 2–3

5 Ready for Chapters Grades 2–4

US $4.99 / $6.50 CAN
ISBN 978-1-101-93492-0

5 0 4 9 9

F&P TEXT LEVEL

RANDOM HOUSE
StepIntoReading.com
Seussville.com
pbskids.org/catinthehat

9 781101 934920